BESHLIE'S
COUNTRYSIDE

To Jean Latter and Ann James

Published in association with

The National Trust
36 Queen Anne's Gate, London SW1 9AS

First published in Great Britain in 1988 by
ORCHARD BOOKS
10 Golden Square, London W1R 3AF
Orchard Books Australia
14 Mars Road, Lane Cove NSW 2066
Orchard Books Canada
20 Torbay Road, Markham, Ontario 23P 1G6
Published in association with Gallery Five
121 King Street, Hammersmith, London W6 9JG
1 85213 043 1
Typeset in Great Britain by P4 Graphics
Printed in Great Britain by Purnell Book Production

BESHLIE'S
COUNTRYSIDE

THE BOOK OF

The Brickmakers,
Farrier &
Drystone-Dyker

ORCHARD BOOKS
in association with *The National Trust*
London

Long-tailed Fieldmice   Round-leaved Mint
Watermint   Wild (or Norse) Mint
Tansy   Water Forget-me-not
Soft Rush   Hard Rush
Herald Moth

8

The Brickmakers

Itinerant families would set up their temporary abode, a simple shelter, thatched with reed or rushes. This was often by the edge of a river, where beds of clay and sand were exposed. The whole family made bricks from these three convenient materials.

Where villages were being built, the Brickmaker and his family were welcome to 'bide a-while'. After completing their task, and before moving on, they left the villagers a pile of bricks for repairs. Many stone or flint cottages have brick corners, chimneys and bread ovens.

Barefoot children removed any stones and stamped the clay, then the men turned and mixed it with sand and water. The women filled *wooden moulds* which had no base, but a movable bottom board. The bricks were turned out from the moulds and stacked in headers and streachers which allowed passage of air. They were then left to dry in the sun.

A *wooden spade,* tipped with metal, was used to dig out the clay, which was less likely to stick to wood. A piece of cloth or strong sacking, called a *cott*, was used on either hand when lifting the finished

brick mould

spade

metal

cott

bricks. The hard sandy edges were abrasive. In the main picture the Brickmaker's wife is wearing one as she turns out a brick.

Clay is the product of rock, decayed and weathered, and millions of years old. It is a heavy material, so the Brickmaker came to the clay for practical reasons.

Chemicals, such as magnesium, carbon and iron give the various clays their colours. Coarse, sandy river clay was used for bricks, white china clay for plates. Each clay has a use, but sometimes they were mixed. Earthenware and pots were glazed.

11

Short-tailed Vole   Betony
Purple Toadflax   Pale Toadflax
Wild Carrot

12

The Farrier

The Worshipful Company of Blacksmiths was founded in 1571. 'By hammer and hand all arts do stand.' Blacksmith is an umbrella title that covers the wrought-iron smith, the blacksmith, and the farrier, who specialises in shoeing horses.

Like toenails, a horse's hoof continues to grow. The iron shoe must be periodically taken off and the hoof cut or 'pared'. This is done with a curved *knife* with a curled top.

If a horse is worked on hard surfaces, the hoof will wear down more quickly than it

grows. Different kinds of iron *shoes* prevent this. Heavy workhorses need heavy shoes, but a racehorse needs a light-weight plate.

Hot-shoeing is best. When the Farrier places the hot shoe against the hoof, there is a cloud of pungent smelling smoke. The shoe burns a pattern, and by the evenness of this the Farrier can see if it will be a perfect fit. If it is not he may need to file off a little more hoof with the coarse *rasp*.

shoes

farrier's knife

To hold the shoes in place, square-sided nails are carefully driven through the outer, insensitive wall of the hoof.

14

heavy coarse teeth

smith's rasp

tongs

As each one emerges, it is twisted off and the end banged over.

In the large picture, the Farrier is looking at a shoe he is making by hammering a strip of iron round the pointed end of his anvil. Behind his head are leather bellows used to keep the forge fire hot. These have a weight at one side so that they can be used by one hand. I used to work these bellows for my grandfather.

A large oak tree often grew outside a Blacksmith's forge, to shelter the horses waiting their turn to be shod.

pincers

Bank Vole   Tufted Vetch
Bramble   Meadow Sweet
Ichneumon Fly   Leopard Moth

16

The Drystone-Dyker

Wherever there is granite, slate, limestone, Cotswold stone, gritstone or sandstone, as in parts of the West Country, Wales, Scotland, the Cotswolds and the Lake District, drystone boundary walls, doubling as windbreaks, have been and still are being built.

Each wall fulfils the need of the immediate environment, and type of local livestock. The name drystone means just what it says, only dry stones are used, no mortar as with bricks. The walls hold together by their shape and the skill of the

17

Dyker or wall-builder's construction.

On bleak, windswept, treeless moorland, walls prevent flocks from mixing, while affording shelter in bad weather. Single walls have stones which go all the way through, and are topped by copers or *combers* — heavy stones which keep the lower ones in place. In the main picture the Dyker is laying one of these.

castle combers

18

mason's hammer

crowbar

A taller, stronger wall had two walls of stone, with the space between filled with hearting or small stone chips. This is known as a *double wall*. Occasionally a large stone is placed all the way through for strength.

The Dyker may use two lines of string and wooden stakes to guide him when building a new wall, or repairing one which is badly damaged.

19

All walls have a wide base tapering to the top. Water must drain off, because when water freezes in a stone, it expands and shatters the stone.

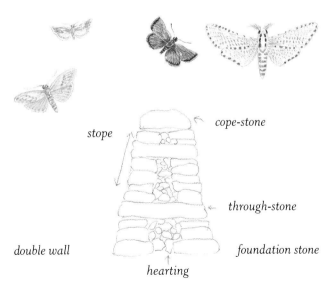

stope

cope-stone

through-stone

double wall

foundation stone

hearting

20

turf

herringbone

To stop cattle jumping over, stones were set on their edge and placed on top. These were called *random stones*. One pattern is called castle — one upright stone, one lying down, alternately.

In some West Country walls the stones are laid in a *herringbone pattern*, and earth is placed on top. Grass and flowers soon colonize this.

random stones